Brown Recluse
SPIDERS

by Eric Ethan

Gareth Stevens Publishing
A WORLD ALMANAC EDUCATION GROUP COMPANY

Please visit our web site at: www.garethstevens.com
For a free color catalog describing Gareth Stevens Publishing's
list of high-quality books and multimedia programs,
call 1-800-542-2595 (USA) or 1-800-387-3178 (Canada).
Gareth Stevens Publishing's fax: (414) 332-3567.

Library of Congress Cataloging-in-Publication Data

Ethan, Eric.
      Brown recluse spiders / by Eric Ethan.
         p. cm. — (Dangerous spiders—an imagination library series)
      Summary: An introduction to the physical characteristics, behavior, and life cycle of
   brown recluse spiders.
      Includes bibliographical references and index.
      ISBN 0-8368-3766-5 (lib. bdg.)
      1. Brown recluse spider—Juvenile literature. [1. Brown recluse spider. 2. Spiders.] I. Title.
   QL458.42.L6E84   2003
   595.4'4—dc21
                                                          2003045556

First published in 2004 by
Gareth Stevens Publishing
A World Almanac Education Group Company
330 West Olive Street, Suite 100
Milwaukee, WI 53212 USA

Text: Eric Ethan
Cover design and page layout: Scott M. Krall
Text editor: Susan Ashley
Series editor: Dorothy L. Gibbs
Picture research: Todtri Book Publishers

Photo credits: Cover © Gary W. Sargent; pp. 5, 13 © James E. Gerholdt; pp. 7, 9, 11, 15, 17
© Rick Vetter; p. 19 © SIU/Visuals Unlimited; p. 21 © Rob & Ann Simpson

Printed in the United States of America

1 2 3 4 5 6 7 8 9 07 06 05 04 03

**Front cover: A brown recluse spider is a
shy creature. Outdoors, its hiding places
include piles of wood, rocks, or leaves.**

TABLE OF CONTENTS

Words that appear in the glossary are printed in **boldface**
type the first time they occur in the text.

BROWN RECLUSE SPIDERS

Some people think that, to be dangerous, a spider has to be **aggressive**. Not the brown recluse spider! The brown recluse is a **timid** creature, yet it is one of the most dangerous spiders in the United States. The **venom**, or poison, in its bite can make people very sick. Some have even died from it.

Fortunately, brown recluse spiders are not very aggressive. They spend most of their time hiding. Even when they feel threatened, they usually run away. Normally, a brown recluse will bite only when it is cornered and has no chance to escape.

Like all spiders, a brown recluse has eight legs, and its body is divided into two parts. All of its legs are attached to the front part of its body.

WHAT THEY LOOK LIKE

Fully grown, a female brown recluse is about the size of a quarter. An adult male is only half that size. Fine hairs cover the bodies and legs of both males and females.

Although their name calls them "brown," these spiders range in color from tan to dark brown. At the front of their bodies, both males and females have a dark brown mark that is shaped like a violin. Because of this mark, brown recluse spiders are also known as "fiddleback" or "violin" spiders.

Another way scientists identify a brown recluse is by counting its eyes. Most spiders have eight eyes, but a brown recluse has only six.

A brown recluse's six eyes look like three pairs of black-rimmed dots arranged in a semicircle on the front part of the spider's body.

HOW THEY GROW

A brown recluse spider begins life as a tiny white egg. A female brown recluse lays about forty eggs at a time. She will produce as many as three hundred eggs in her lifetime, which is about two years.

Females lay most of their eggs between May and August. They wrap the eggs in balls of silk called egg sacs and hang the egg sacs in their webs, where they guard them until the eggs are ready to hatch. In warm weather, the eggs usually hatch in three to five weeks. Egg sacs that are produced in autumn, when the air is cooler, might not hatch until warm weather returns the following spring.

The silk threads that form the egg sac of a brown recluse spider are woven very loosely, so the little round eggs inside it are easy to see.

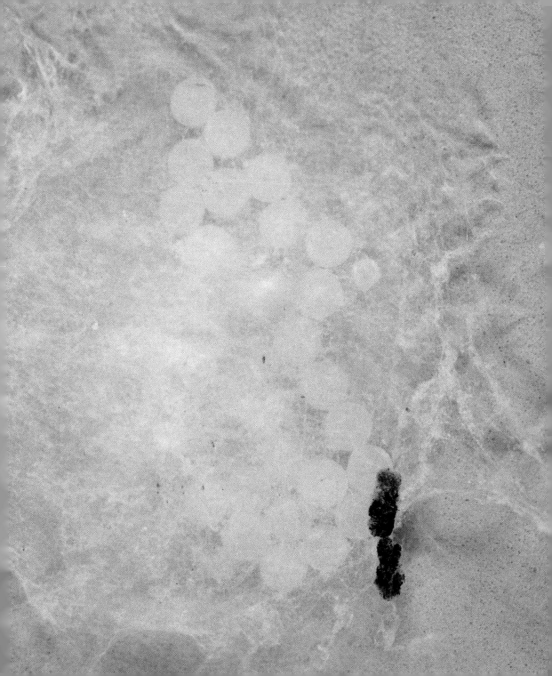

The baby spiders are called spiderlings. When they come out of the egg sac, they are not fully grown. It takes ten to twelve months for brown recluse spiderlings to grow to their full adult size. Once they are fully grown, they might live one more year.

In order to grow, a brown recluse has to **molt**, or shed its outer covering. Like all spiders, the brown recluse has a hard shell called a **carapace** covering its body. As the spider's body grows, however, its protective shell does not. When the shell becomes too small, it breaks open, and the spider crawls out. Gradually, a new shell hardens around the spider's body. Spiderlings molt several times before they become adults.

When a brown recluse spider molts, its hard shell splits into two pieces so the spider is able to crawl out. The broken shell is left behind.

WHERE THEY LIVE

Brown recluse spiders live mainly in the south-central part of the United States. North to south, their range is from southern Iowa to Louisiana. East to west, they are found from Kentucky to Oklahoma.

These spiders make their homes in quiet, sheltered places. Outdoors, they weave their webs underneath rocks or in woodpiles. Indoors, they are most often found in basements or closets, inside storage boxes, or under furniture. Sometimes, they even hide in dresser drawers. Brown recluse spiders are attracted to people's homes because houses have lots of warm, dry places, which is what these spiders like best.

This brown recluse has a light brown body and dark brown legs. These colors help the spider blend into its woodland surroundings.

THEIR WEBS

The web of a brown recluse spider is small, loose, and shapeless. It is made of silk threads that the spider produces inside its body. The silk comes out of small openings, called **spinnerets**, at the back of the spider's **abdomen**.

Unlike the kinds of spiders that use their webs to trap food, brown recluse spiders use their webs for shelter. They like to stay out of sight during the day, and their webs are safe places to hide. Their webs are also safe places for their eggs. When a female brown recluse is guarding her egg sacs, she rarely leaves her web.

The web of a brown recluse spider is known as a sheet web. The silk is loosely woven in a patternless mass that is flat, like a blanket.

HUNTING FOR FOOD

A hungry brown recluse goes out to eat! It does not stay home waiting for food to get caught in its web. This spider is a **nocturnal** hunter, which means that it leaves its web at night to search for food.

Brown recluse spiders like to eat insects, especially cockroaches. When a brown recluse sees something to eat, it acts quickly — first, **pouncing** on the **prey**, then biting it. The spider's **fangs inject** a poison, or venom, that kills the insect. The fangs also inject special juices that turn the insect's body tissues into a liquid. Then, like other spiders, the brown recluse "drinks" its meal.

Brown recluse spiders are hunters rather than trappers. They leave their webs to find food. This brown recluse is eating a cricket.

THEIR BITES

Both male and female brown recluse spiders are poisonous. A bite from either one can be very serious, especially for young children and elderly adults. How serious a bite is depends on how much venom is injected and how sensitive the person is to the venom. Some people do not even realize they have been bitten until after a few hours. By then, the area around the bite is probably red and swollen, because this spider's venom attacks body tissues.

At the present time, there is no **antivenin** for brown recluse bites, but doctors have other kinds of treatments that help relieve the effects of the poison.

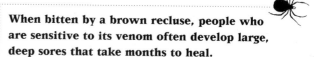

When bitten by a brown recluse, people who are sensitive to its venom often develop large, deep sores that take months to heal.

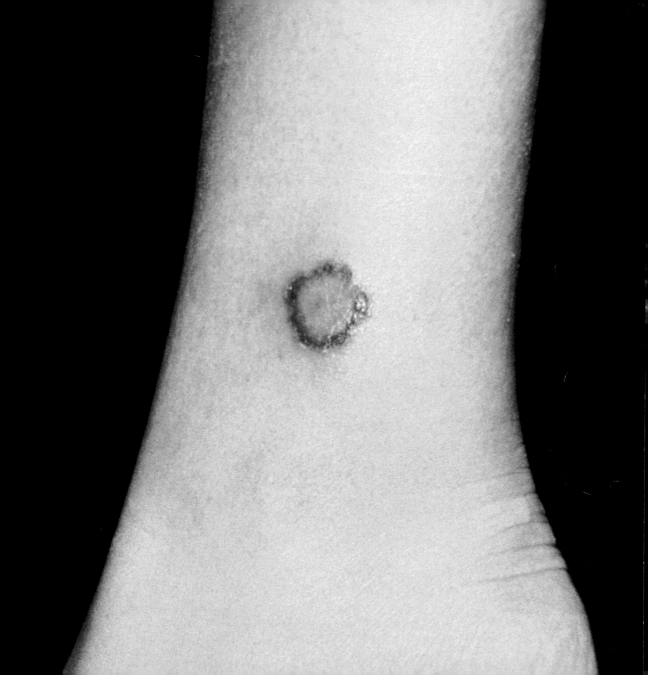

THEIR ENEMIES

Birds, insects, and even other spiders prey on the brown recluse, especially on the spiderlings. Many spiderlings die before they are fully grown. But the greatest enemy of the brown recluse is human.

People do not want to share their homes with dangerous spiders, so they kill any they find. They usually use chemical sprays to clear the spiders out of their houses or any other buildings where a brown recluse has taken up **residence**.

If you find one brown recluse in the house, there are probably more. The best time to look for them is at night — but not with bare feet!

MORE TO READ AND VIEW

Books (Nonfiction)
About Arachnids: A Guide for Children. Cathryn P. Sill (Peachtree)
Life Cycle of a Spider. Ron Fridell and Patricia Walsh
    (Heinemann Library)
Misunderstood: Spiders. John L'Hommedieu (Child's Play International)
Spider. Killer Creatures (series). David Jefferis and Tony Allan
    (Raintree/Steck-Vaughn)
The Spider. Life Cycles (series). Sabrina Crewe (Raintree)
Spiders. Secret World of (series). Theresa Greenaway (Raintree)
Spiders and Their Kin. A Golden Guide (series). Herbert Walter Levi
    and Lorna Rose Levi (Golden Books)
Spiders Spin Webs. Yvonne Winer (Charlesbridge)

Books (Fiction)
Charlotte's Web. E. B. White (HarperCollins)
Once I Knew a Spider. Jennifer Owings Dewey (Walker & Co.)
The Spider and the Fly. Mary Botham Howitt (Simon & Schuster)
Spider Weaver: A Legend of Kente. Margaret Musgrove and Julia
    Caims (Scholastic)

Videos (Nonfiction)
Bug City: Spiders & Scorpions. (Schlessinger Media)
Nightmares of Nature: Spider Attack. (National Geographic)
See How They Grow: Insects & Spiders. (Sony Wonder)

WEB SITES

Web sites change frequently, so one or more of the following recommended sites may no longer be available. To find more information about brown recluse spiders, you can also use a good search engine, such as **Yahooligans!** [www.yahooligans.com] or Google [www.google.com]. Here are some keywords to help you: *brown recluse, poisonous spiders, recluse spiders, spider bites.*

kidshealth.org/kid/ill_injure/aches/brown_recluse.html

"Hey! A Brown Recluse Spider Bit Me!" is part of the information-packed *KidsHealth* web site. It is the first in a series of pages that are dedicated to information about the bite of a brown recluse spider. After learning about the spider, you can click on links to "What a Brown Recluse Spider Bite Looks and Feels Like" and "What a Doctor Will Do." All of the information has been reviewed by qualified medical doctors.

polk.ga.net/Westside/Spider/Westside_Spidermania.html

Small line drawings and some very nice close-up photographs accompany brief paragraphs of basic information about brown recluse spiders, as well as black widows, tarantulas, and four other eight-legged creepy crawlers. Although the facts are brief, having similar information for seven different spiders, side by side, comes in handy when you want to make comparisons.

www.art-teenz.tv/template/amazingfacts/amazingfacts_insectbites.asp

Here's another interesting site for making comparisons. This time, you can compare insect bites. Of course, you know that spiders are not insects, but, since they bite and sting like insects, *art Teenz.tv* has included black widows and brown recluse spiders on its "Insect-bites" top ten. Along with a line drawing and the description of each insect (or spider), this listing also provides a brief description of that creature's bite.

www.uky.edu/Agriculture/CritterFiles/casefile/spiders/brownspider/brownspider.htm

In the "Critter Case Files" on the University of Kentucky's *Entomology for Kids* web site, the brown recluse is simply known as a brown spider. The case file presents brief but well-organized information, ranging from how to identify a brown recluse to its "pest status." This site also distinguishes fact from folklore.

GLOSSARY

You will find these words on the page or pages listed after each definition.
Reading a word in a sentence can help you understand it even better.

abdomen (AB-doh-men) — the back half of a spider's body, which contains its spinnerets, eggs, heart, lungs, and other organs 14

aggressive (uh-GRES-iv) — bold and forceful, usually the first to attack or start a fight 4

antivenin (an-tee-VEN-in) — a kind of medicine that helps prevent venom from causing painful wounds, illness, or death 18

carapace (KARE-ah-pace) — the hard shell that covers and protects the soft body of an animal and the organs inside it 10

fangs (FANGZ) — long, pointed teeth 16

inject (in-JEKT) — to force a liquid into body tissues through a sharp, pointed, needlelike instrument 16, 18

molt (MOHLT) — to shed a covering, such as skin, on the outside of the body 10

nocturnal (nock-TER-nel) — active during the night and at rest during the day 16

pouncing (POUN-sing) — leaping, suddenly, on top of something, usually to capture it 16

prey (PRAY) — (n) an animal that is killed by another animal for food 16; (v) to hunt and kill for food 20

residence (REZ-ih-dents) — the act of living in a place as a home 20

spinnerets (spin-nuh-RETS) — fingerlike organs at the back of a spider's abdomen, which the spider uses to make silk 14

timid (TIM-id) — shy and fearful 4

venom (VEN-um) — poison that an animal produces in its body and passes into a victim by biting or stinging 4, 16, 18

INDEX